Convinced by the Word

Healed by God

by

E. Michal Gayer

...being fully persuaded, that what He had promised
He was also able to perform.

Romans 4:21

He sent His word, and healed them....

Psalm 107:20

Unless otherwise indicated, all Scripture quotations in this book are from the *King James Version* of the Bible.

CONVINCED BY THE WORD, HEALED BY GOD
Copyright ©1995 by E. Michal Gayer

First printing, October 1996
Second printing, September 2001
Third printing, August 2003

ISBN 0-9654759-0-5

Published by
LIGHTSHINE ROCK PUBLISHERS
P.O. Box 225
Stuarts Draft, VA 24477

DEDICATED

To Elizabeth and Steve Bahorik, my mother and father, whose love and faith led me to Jesus Christ.

To my husband Bob through whose love and faith my own has prospered and grown.

To my sons, Robbyn and Brett, whose love and faith has added meaning and delight to my life.

To my brothers, Stephen and Wesley Bahorik, and their families whose love and faith has encouraged and sustained me.

To all Christians who through love and faith seek a closer relationship with Jesus Christ.

About the Author

E. Michal Gayer writes from a unique background of deep involvement in church ministry work after departing from a successful career as a Christian psychologist. Her education and training afford the exceptional combination of her having a well-developed understanding of human personality, character and relationships as well as a deep and rich grasp of Christian ministry work. She holds a Bachelor of Arts Degree from Juniata College, a Master of Arts Degree in Clinical Psychology from Wayne State University, and has pursued studies through Life Bible College and the Shenandoah Bible Institute. Professional licenses which she has received during her lifetime include Staff & District Ministerial Licenses from the Southeast District of the Church of the Foursquare Gospel, International Ministerial License with the International Church of the Foursquare Gospel, Psychologist License (PA) and Psychological Diagnostician License (MI).

Her ministry work includes teaching and preaching as well as developing and administrating specialized Christian ministry and educational programs. These programs have focused mainly on the needs of individuals who are sick and in need of healing. Hundreds of volunteers as well as thousands of respondents have ministered to the sick through these Christian prayer, support and outreach programs. Michal is the Founding Director of the Healing Rooms of Augusta County, VA. Other experiences she has had include having worked as a School Psychologist, Clinical Staff Psychologist, Business Consultant, and College Instructor at Henry Ford Community College, the Pennsylvania State University Pittsburgh Extension and Blue Ridge Community College. She has also taught at the Mary Baldwin College Adult Community Learning Center, is an author, has written numerous newspaper articles and is both a guest lecturer and guest preacher.

Having grown up in Pennsylvania in a loving, devoutly Christian home with her parents and two older brothers, E. Michal Gayer currently lives in Virginia with her husband Robert and their two sons Robbyn and Brett.

CONTENTS

INTRODUCTION

One of the key aspects of God's relationship with mankind is reflected in His statement, "I am the Lord that healeth thee." (Exodus 15:26). Not only did God speak this awesome declaration but He also enforced it by making provisions to heal people of all manner of sickness and disease. The reality of this has been evidenced throughout history with the most profound revelation expressed through the life, death, and resurrection of Jesus Christ, "...by whose stripes ye were healed." (I Peter 2:24).

God's divine healing plan, encompassing the many powerful concepts detailing God's way to divine healing, is recorded throughout the pages of the Bible as a rich and glorious gift from God. Every book of the Bible, in one way or another, contains elements of that plan conveyed either through specific promises and instructions given by God or from a broader perspective through His revealed relationship with mankind.

The opportunity to glean from the Word of God the essential truths and understandings pertaining to God's way to healing is an impressive privilege to all people, but because of the complexities involved concerning sickness and disease and the importance of having an obedient walk with God, it is likewise a serious mandate. God calls us through the inspiration of Proverbs 4:20-22 to "...attend to my words; incline thine ear unto my sayings. Let them not depart from thine eyes; keep them in the midst of thine heart. For they are life unto those that find them, and health to all their flesh." A persistent devotion to and faithfulness to God's Word is, therefore, significant in order for the truths inherent in it to be successfully applied and the fullness of God's benefits received.

Since healing scripture passages are scattered throughout the Bible, it is often difficult and time consuming to locate specific verses quickly and efficiently. This handbook represents a compiling of key scripture verses pertaining to divine healing. It has been created to serve as an easy access guide to healing scripture and should prove useful as a resource tool. When immediate recall of specific healing scripture verses are needed, as is frequently necessary for personal reference, when ministering to the sick, or for other aspects of ministry work, this handbook could prove to be invaluable.

The collection of healing scripture verses in this handbook, while comprehensive, is not intended in any way to replace necessary, diligent and thorough Bible study. Likewise, it should not be used as a "formula for healing", or a substitute for developing the essential personal relationship with God through Jesus Christ which is so vital to the healing process and every other aspect of life as well. When properly used, this handbook will provide quick access to key healing scripture verses and will be a valuable and convenient resource under many circumstances.

Special attention should be paid to the table of contents. It has been developed and organized in outline form to touch on some of the most significant aspects of divine healing. The main categories and their related subcategory statements are intended to serve as a guide for the serious reader to the scripture verses provided throughout the handbook. The result, hopefully, will be the emergence of a general overview and understanding of God's divine healing plan.

I

THE WORD OF GOD IS TRUSTWORTHY AND EVERLASTING

The Bible, as the written Word of God, was developed by the inspiration of the Holy Spirit who moved on prophets, apostles, and other holy men of God to record God's revelation of Himself, His purpose and His plans to people. Through the recorded account of these spokespeople, God has used the Bible as a primary means of making Himself known to mankind. All scripture is given by inspiration of God and is potentially profitable to instruct, encourage, correct and equip people as they develop a relationship with Him (II Timothy 3:16).

A life lived in accordance with God's will that is blessed by Him requires an acceptance, belief in and adherence to God's Word as recorded in the Bible. God and His Word are one (I John 5:7). When God speaks forth His Word, it accomplishes what He says it will accomplish (Isaiah 55:11) because His Word is living and powerful (Hebrews 4:12).

God's Word is the avenue for the development of faith (Romans 10:17) and plays a key role in divine healing (Psalm 107:20). His Word reveals not only His divine healing plan in general but it also offers assurances, promises, instructions and requirements specific to receiving healing from God. This first section of the handbook will focus mainly on the validity and importance of the Word of God. More specific expansion on God's divine healing plan will be developed in later sections.

1. The Word of God is eternal.

John 1:1 In the beginning was the Word, and the Word was with God, and the Word was God.

I Peter 1:25 ...the word of the Lord endureth for ever.

Isaiah 40:8 The grass withereth, the flower fadeth: but the word of our God shall stand for ever.

Matthew 24:35 Heaven and earth shall pass away, but my words shall not pass away.

Psalm 119:89 For ever, O Lord, thy word is settled in heaven.

2. God's Word is sovereign and accomplishes God's purposes.

I John 5:7 For there are three that bear record in heaven, the Father, the Word, and the Holy Ghost: and these three are one.

Psalm 138:2-3 ...thou hast magnified thy word above all thy name.
   In the day when I cried thou answeredst me, and strengthenedst me with strength in my soul.

Psalm 89:34 My covenant will I not break, nor alter the thing that is gone out of my lips.

Isaiah 55:11 So shall my word be that goeth

forth out of my mouth: it shall not return unto me void, but it shall accomplish that which I please, and it shall prosper in the thing whereto I sent it.

Ezekiel 12:25 For I am the Lord: I will speak, and the word that I shall speak shall come to pass; it shall be no more prolonged: for in your days, O rebellious house, will I say the word, and will perform it, saith the Lord God.

Ezekiel 12:28 Therefore say unto them, Thus saith the Lord God; There shall none of my words be prolonged any more, but the word which I have spoken shall be done, saith the Lord God.

Jeremiah 1:12 Then said the Lord unto me, Thou hast well seen: for I will hasten my word to perform it.

3. God's Word is powerful and useful.

Hebrews 4:12 For the word of God is quick, and powerful, and sharper than any two-edged sword, piercing even to the dividing asunder of soul and spirit, and of the joints and marrow, and is a discerner of the thoughts and intents of the heart.

II Timothy 3:16,17 All scripture is given by inspiration of God, and is profitable for doctrine, for reproof, for correction, for instruction in righteousness:
That the man of God may be perfect, thoroughly furnished unto all good works.

Matthew 4:4 ...It is written, Man shall not live by bread alone, but by every word that proceedeth out of the mouth of God.

Romans 10:17 ...faith cometh by hearing, and hearing by the word of God.

Proverbs 4:20-22 My son, attend to my words; incline thine ear unto my sayings.

Let them not depart from thine eyes; keep them in the midst of thine heart.

For they are life unto those that find them, and health to all their flesh.

Psalm 107:20 He sent his word, and healed them, and delivered them from their destructions.

4. God's Word never fails!

I Kings 8:56 Blessed be the Lord, that hath given rest unto his people Israel, according to all that he promised: there hath not failed one word of all his good promise, which he promised by the hand of Moses his servant.

Joshua 21:45 There failed not aught of any good thing which the Lord had spoken unto the house of Israel; all came to pass.

Numbers 23:19 God is not a man, that he should lie; neither the son of man, that he should repent: hath he said, and shall he not do it? or hath he spoken, and shall he not make it good?

Romans 3:4 ...let God be true, but every man a liar...

II

THE SUPERSTRUCTURE OF DIVINE HEALING IS ONE GOD REVEALED IN THREE PERSONS

There is only one God, the creator of heaven and earth. No other God existed before Him nor will another God come after Him (Isaiah 43:10). Coexistent in perfect harmony and unity within the one God are three distinct persons: the Father, the Son and the Holy Spirit (I John 5:7; John 1:1-18).

God the Father has revealed Himself to be all powerful, all knowing, omnipresent, changeless and eternal. He is the source of ultimate truth and His essential nature is love. Motivated by love, He sent His only begotten Son Jesus Christ to redeem and reconcile sinful mankind back to Himself.

The Son Jesus Christ in obedience to the Father assumed human flesh and suffered death, even the death of the cross, to set mankind free from the bondage and slavery of sin (Phillipians 2:6-11). Redemption and salvation were fully accomplished when Jesus Christ rose from the dead victorious over sin and death. Through belief in Him all mankind has the opportunity to be born again into the family of God and become heirs to eternal life.

The Holy Spirit, the third person of the Godhead, is coexistent and eternal with the Father and the Son. Promised by the

Father, the Holy Spirit was sent by Jesus Christ after His final ascension to the Father. The Holy Spirit came to indwell individual believers and endue them with power. As the personal "Helper" to all believers, the Holy Spirit exercises and demonstrates God's power in their lives. To an unbelieving world the Holy Spirit has come to convict the world of sin, righteousness and judgement as He actively participates in God's salvation plan (John 16:8-15). Moving in complete unity and harmony with the Father and the Son, the Holy Spirit is God's agent of power on earth today.

Concerning divine healing, all three persons of the Godhead play a vital role. The interworking of Father, Son and Holy Spirit forms the superstructure for divine healing as revealed in the Bible. This majestic reality will be expanded upon more fully in the following sections of this handbook.

5. There is one God revealed in three persons.

Deuteronomy 6:4-5 Hear, O Israel: The Lord our God is one Lord:
And thou shalt love the Lord thy God with all thine heart, and with all thy soul, and with all thy might.

Isaiah 43:10 ...before me there was no God formed, neither shall there be after me.

Isaiah 43:11 I, even I, am the Lord; and beside me there is no savior.

Isaiah 44:8 ...Is there a God besides me? yea, there is no God; I know not any.

I Timothy 2:5-6 For there is one God, and one mediator between God and men, the man Christ Jesus;

Who gave himself a ransom for all...

Ephesians 2:18 For through him we both have access by one Spirit unto the Father.

I John 5:7 For there are three that bear record in heaven, the Father, the Word, and the Holy Ghost: and these three are one.

Ephesians 4:4-6 There is one body, and one Spirit, even as ye are called in one hope of your calling;

One Lord, one faith, one baptism,

One God and Father of all, who is above all, and through all, and in you all.

II Corinthians 13:14 The grace of the Lord Jesus Christ, and the love of God, and the communion of the Holy Ghost, be with you all. Amen.

Matthew 28:19 Go ye therefore and teach all nations, baptizing them in the name of the Father, and of the Son, and of the Holy Ghost;

I Corinthians 12:4-6 Now there are diversities of gifts, but the same Spirit.

And there are differences of administrations, but the same Lord.

And there are diversities of operations, but it is the same God which worketh all in all.

6. God the Father, Jesus the Son and the Holy Spirit all participate in divine healing.

Acts 10:38 ...God anointed Jesus of Nazareth with the Holy Ghost and with power: who went about doing good, and healing all that were oppressed of the devil; for God was with him.

Exodus 15:26 ...the voice of the Lord thy God...for I am the Lord that healeth thee.

Exodus 23:25 And ye shall serve the Lord your God, and he shall bless thy bread, and thy water; and I will take sickness away from the midst of thee.

Matthew 9:35 And Jesus went about all the cities and villages, teaching in their synagogues, and preaching the gospel of the kingdom, and healing every sickness, and every disease among the people.

I Peter 2:24 ...his own self bare our sins in his own body on the tree, that we, being dead to sins, should live unto righteousness: by whose stripes ye were healed.

Matthew 12:28 But if I cast out devils by the Spirit of God, then the kingdom of God is come unto you.

I Corinthians 12:7,9 But the manifestations of the Spirit is given to every man to profit withal. ...the gifts of healing by the same Spirit.

III

GOD THE FATHER PROVIDES HEALING

The revelation that God's essential nature is love runs throughout the Bible from beginning to end. It is not surprising then that the theme of divine healing also runs like a golden thread throughout the Bible born from and intertwining with this profound truth that "God is love" (I John 4:8).

The whole concept of healing is God's idea not mankinds'. That He built the potential for healing and repair into the cellular structure of the human body, has inspired medical advancements and continues to provide supernaturally to heal, attests to His great love for His created beings. Healing is nothing less than a product of God's love!

Although God's role in healing was revealed much earlier, one of the most profound revelations occurred when the Children of Israel were freed from slavery. The first covenant God made with them when they had traveled just a few days beyond the Red Sea was the covenant of healing. He mightily and powerfully declared for all eternity, "...I am the Lord that healeth thee" (Exodus 15:26).

God the Father, the first person of the trinity, is good to His children upholding, protecting and preserving the lives of those who love Him (Psalm 145:20). It is His sovereign will to heal the sick. His divine healing plan to accomplish precisely that has been masterminded, made available and empowered by Him.

"Like as a father pitieth his children, so the Lord pitieth them that fear Him" (Psalm 103:13). He "...forgiveth all thine iniquities" and "...healeth all thy diseases" (Psalm 103:3). As Jesus' Father and the heavenly Father of all who come to Him through Jesus Christ, God the Father stands ready and able to be "...the Lord that healeth..." (Exodus 15:26).

7. God is good to all.

> **Psalm 145:9** The Lord is good to all: and his tender mercies are over all his works.

> **James 1:17** Every good gift and every perfect gift is from above, and cometh down from the Father of lights, with whom is no variableness, neither shadow of turning.

> **Psalm 84:11** For the Lord God is a sun and shield: the Lord will give grace and glory; no good thing will he withhold from them that walk uprightly.

8. God upholds, protects, and preserves the lives of those who love Him and meet the conditions of His promises.

> **Psalm 145:20** The Lord preserveth all them that love him: but all the wicked will he destroy.

> **Isaiah 41:10** Fear thou not; for I am with thee: be not dismayed; for I am thy God: I will strengthen thee; yea, I will help thee; yea I will uphold thee with the right hand of my righteousness.

Psalm 42:11 Why art thou cast down, O my soul? and why art thou disquieted within me? hope thou in God: for I shall yet praise him, who is the health of my countenance, and my God.

Psalm 91:15-16 He shall call upon me, and I will answer him: I will be with him in trouble; I will deliver him, and honour him.

With long life will I satisfy him, and shew him my salvation.

Psalm 91:10 There shall no evil befall thee, neither shall any plague come nigh thy dwelling.

2 Peter 3:9 The Lord is not slack concerning his promise, as some men count slackness; but is long-suffering to us-ward not willing that any should perish, but that all should come to repentance.

Psalm 34:10 The young lions do lack, and suffer hunger: but they that seek the Lord shall not want any good thing.

Psalm 128:1 Blessed is every one that feareth the Lord; that walketh in his ways.

Malachi 4:2 But unto you that fear my name, shall the Sun of righteousness arise with healing in his wings...

Hebrews 11:6 ...he that cometh to God must believe that he is, and that he is a rewarder of them that diligently seek him.

9. It is God's will to heal.

Exodus 15:26 ...I am the Lord that healeth thee.

Psalm 103:2-3 Bless the Lord, O my soul, and forget not all his benefits:
Who forgiveth all thine iniquities; who healeth all thy diseases;

Deuteronomy 7:15 And the Lord will take away from thee all sickness...

Exodus 23:25 And ye shall serve the Lord your God, and he shall bless thy bread, and thy water; and I will take sickness away from the midst of thee.

Jeremiah 30:17 For I will restore health unto thee, and I will heal thee of thy wounds, saith the Lord;

Psalm 147:3 He healeth the broken in heart, and bindeth up their wounds.

Jeremiah 33:6 Behold, I will bring it health and cure, and I will cure them, and will reveal unto them the abundance of peace and truth.

II Chronicles 30:20 And the Lord hearkened to Hezekiah, and healed the people.

Psalm 30:2 O Lord my God, I cried unto thee, and thou hast healed me.

Jeremiah 17:14 Heal me, O Lord, and I shall be healed; save me, and I shall be saved: for thou art my praise.

Psalm 107:20 He sent his word, and healed them, and delivered them from their destructions.

Malachi 4:2 But unto you that fear my name, shall the Sun of righteousness arise with healing in his wings; and ye shall go forth, and grow up as calves of the stall.

III John 1:2 Beloved, I wish above all things that thou mayest prosper and be in health, even as thy soul prospereth.

IV

JESUS IS CHRIST THE HEALER

Jesus Christ, who is the Son of the living God and the second person of the trinity, was sent by God as an expression of His generosity and love toward the family of mankind. When Jesus, "...was made flesh, and dwelt among us..." (John 1:14), He came as the most perfect revelation of God the Father. Jesus Himself said, "...He that believeth on me, believeth not on me, but on him who sent me: And he that seeth me, seeth him that sent me" (John 12:44-45). He also stated, "For I have not spoken of myself, but the Father which sent me, he gave me a commandment, what I should say, and what I should speak" (John 12:49). Accordingly, Jesus was the ultimate expression of God speaking only those words given by the Father. In a like manner, the actions he took were in accordance with and demonstrated God's will. Jesus clearly stated this as recorded in John 6:38, "For I came down from heaven, not to do mine own will, but the will of him that sent me."

During His earthly ministry Jesus proclaimed the presence of the kingdom of God and went about "...doing good, and healing all who were oppressed by the devil; for God was with him" (Acts 10:38). Healing the sick was a vital part of Jesus' ministry. He healed "...all manner of sickness, and all manner of disease among the people" (Matthew 4:23). Matthew 12:15 records that even great multitudes followed Him and "...he healed them all."

As Jesus ministered to sick people healing them of all kinds of sickness and disease and healing multitudes of sick people who came to Him, He revealed another major portion of God's divine healing provisions for mankind. As the One who was sent by God, Jesus revealed for the world to clearly see that it is God's will that people should receive healing from all and every kind of sickness. Every person who is sick can turn to God with great confidence and assurance that it is God's will to heal and that divine healing has been made available for them to receive through His Son Jesus Christ.

10. Jesus was sent by God to perform the will of the Father.

John 3:16 For God so loved the world, that he gave his only begotten Son, that whosoever believeth in him should not perish, but have everlasting life.

Matthew 16:13, 15-16 When Jesus came unto the coasts of Cesarea Philippi, he asked his disciples, saying, Whom do men say that I, the Son of man, am?

He saith unto them, But whom say ye that I am?

And Simon Peter answered and said, Thou art the Christ, the Son of the living God.

John 6:38 For I came down from heaven, not to do mine own will, but the will of him that sent me.

Colossians 2:9-10 For in him dwelleth all the fullness of the Godhead bodily.

And ye are complete in him, which is the head of all principality and power:

Hebrews 10:9 Then he said, Lo, I come to do thy will, O God. He taketh away the first, that he may establish the second.

John 12:49-50 For I have not spoken of myself; but the Father which sent me, he gave me a commandment, what I should say, and what I should speak.

And I know that his commandment is life everlasting: whatsoever I speak therefore, even as the Father said unto me, so I speak.

John 5:19 Then answered Jesus, and said unto them, Verily, verily, I say unto you, The Son can do nothing of himself, but what he seeth the Father do; for what things soever he doeth, these also doeth the Son likewise.

John 12:44-45 Jesus cried, and said, He that believeth on me, believeth not on me, but on him that sent me:

And he that seeth me, seeth him that sent me:

I John 3:8 He that committeth sin is of the devil; for the devil sinneth from the beginning. For this purpose the Son of God was manifested, that he might destroy the works of the devil.

John 14:6 Jesus saith unto him, I am the way, the truth, and the life: no man cometh unto the Father, but by me.

11. Jesus healed the sick.

Luke 9:11 And the people, when they knew it, followed him: and he received them, and spake unto them of the kingdom of God, and healed them that had need of healing.

Mark 1:34 And he healed many that were sick of divers diseases, and cast out many devils; and suffered not the devils to speak, because they knew him.

Mark 3:10 For he had healed many; insomuch that they pressed upon him for to touch him, as many as had plagues.

Matthew 21:14 And the blind and the lame came to him in the temple; and he healed them.

Matthew 9:20, 22 And behold a woman which was diseased with an issue of blood twelve years, came behind him, and touched the hem of his garment.

But Jesus turned him about, and when he saw her, he said, Daughter, be of good comfort: thy faith hath made thee whole. And the woman was made whole from that hour.

Luke 17:12-14 And as he entered into a certain village, there met him ten men that were lepers, which stood afar off:

And they lifted up their voices, and said, Jesus, Master, have mercy on us.

And when he saw them, he said unto them, Go shew yourselves unto the priests. And it came to pass, that, as they went, they were cleansed.

Mark 10:46, 47, 49, 50, 51, 52 ...blind Bartimeus, the son of Timeus, sat by the high-way side begging.

And when he heard that it was Jesus of Nazareth, he began to cry out, and say, Jesus, thou son of David, have mercy on me.

And Jesus stood still, and commanded him to be called: and they call the blind man, saying unto him, Be of good comfort, rise; he calleth thee.

And he, casting away his garment, rose, and came to Jesus.

And Jesus answered and said unto him, What wilt thou that I should do unto thee? The blind man said unto him, Lord, that I might receive my sight.

And Jesus said unto him, Go thy way; thy faith hath made thee whole. And immediately he received his sight, and followed Jesus in the way.

Mark 3:1,5 And he entered again into the synagogue; and there was a man there which had a withered hand.

...he saith unto the man, Stretch forth thine hand. And he stretched it out: and his hand was restored whole as the other.

Luke 13:11-13 And behold, there was a woman which had a spirit of infirmity eighteen years, and was bowed together, and could in no wise lift up herself.

And when Jesus saw her, he called her to him, and said unto her, Woman, thou art loosed from thine infirmity.

And he laid his hands on her: and immediately she was made straight, and glorified God.

Mark 7:32-35 And they bring unto him one that was deaf, and had an impediment in his speech; and they beseech him to put his hand upon him.

And he took him aside from the multitude, and put his fingers into his ears, and he spit, and touched his tongue:

And looking up to heaven, he sighed, and saith unto him, Ephphatha, that is, Be opened.

And straightway his ears were opened, and the string of his tongue was loosed, and he spake plain.

Matthew 8:2-3 And behold, there came a leper and worshipped him, saying, Lord, if thou wilt, thou canst make me clean.

And Jesus put forth his hand, and touched him, saying, I will; be thou clean. And immediately his leprosy was cleansed.

Matthew 20:30, 34 And behold, two blind men sitting by the way-side, when they heard that Jesus passed by, cried out, saying, Have mercy on us, O Lord, thou son of David.

So Jesus had compassion on them, and touched their eyes: and immediately their eyes received sight, and they followed him.

Matthew 9:18 ...there came a certain ruler, and worshipped him, saying, My daughter is even now dead: but come and lay thy hand upon her, and she shall live.

Matthew 9:23-25 And when Jesus came into the ruler's house, and saw the minstrels and the people making a noise,

He said unto them, Give place: for the maid is not dead, but sleepeth. And they laughed him to scorn.

But when the people were put forth, he went in, and took her by the hand, and the maid arose.

12. It is God's will that all should be healed. Jesus healed everyone who came to him.

Acts 10:38 How God anointed Jesus of Nazareth with the Holy Ghost and with power: who went about doing good, and healing all that were oppressed of the devil; for God was with him.

Matthew 8:16-17 ...they brought unto him many that were possessed with devils: and he cast out the spirits with his word, and healed all that were sick;

That it might be fulfilled which was spoken by Esaias the prophet, saying, Himself took our infirmities, and bare our sicknesses.

Luke 6:19 And the whole multitude sought to touch him; for there went virtue out of him, and healed them all.

Matthew 12:15 But when Jesus knew it, he withdrew himself from thence: and great multitudes followed him, and he healed them all.

Luke 4:40 Now when the sun was setting, all they that had any sick with divers diseases, brought them unto him: and he laid his hands on every one of them, and healed them.

Mark 6:56 And whithersoever he entered, into villages, or cities, or country, they laid the sick in the streets, and besought him that they might touch, if it were but the border of his garment: and as many as touched him, were made whole.

Matthew 14:35-36 ...they sent out into all that country round about, and brought unto him all that were diseased;

And besought him that they might only touch the hem of his garment: and as many as touched were made perfectly whole.

III John 2 Beloved, I wish above all things that thou mayest prosper and be in health, even as thy soul prospereth.

13. Jesus healed every kind of sickness and disease.

Matthew 9:35   And Jesus went about all the cities and villages, teaching in their synagogues, and preaching the gospel of the kingdom, and healing every sickness, and every disease among the people.

Matthew 4:23-24   And Jesus went about all Galilee, teaching in their synagogues, and preaching the gospel of the kingdom, and healing all manner of sickness, and all manner of disease among the people.

And his fame went throughout all Syria: and they brought unto him all sick people that were taken with divers diseases and torments, and those which were possessed with devils, and those which were lunatic, and those that had the palsy; and he healed them.

V

JESUS' AUTHORITY AND THE BELIEVERS' AUTHORITY ARE OVER SICKNESS AND ALL THE POWER OF THE ENEMY

During His earthly ministry Jesus spoke and acted not according to His own unique desires and intents, but on the instructions and authority of God the Father. In the Gospel according to John, Jesus is recorded as saying "...the Son can do nothing of himself, but what he seeth the Father do; for what things soever he doeth, these also doeth the Son likewise...For as the Father hath life in himself, so hath he given to the Son to have life in himself; And hath given him authority...I can of mine own self do nothing: as I hear, I judge: and my judgement is just, because I seek not mine own will, but the will of the Father which hath sent me" (John 5:19, 26-27, 30).

Jesus was sent and fully authorized by God to preach, teach, cast out devils, heal the sick and accomplish all the works that He did during His earthly ministry. Not only was He sent and authorized, He was also fully empowered to accomplish the same. As part of God's long range plan, Jesus passed along to all true believers the authority He had. He gave them the opportunity to be empowered by the Holy Spirit, as He was, and to function in such a way as to carry on with the ministry work He had begun (Matthew 28:18; Luke 9:1-2; Mark 3:14-15; Matthew 10:1; Luke 10:19). As ambassadors for Christ (II Corinthians 5:20), sons of God (Romans 8:14) and joint heirs with Jesus

Christ (Romans 8:17), believers are to receive most seriously the instructions Jesus gave when He said, "Verily, verily, I say unto you, He that believeth on me, the works that I do shall he do also; and greater works than these he will do; because I go unto my Father" (John 14:12).

Healing the sick was a major work of Jesus, one which He commissioned believers to participate in and accomplish. In awesome, authoritative directives to believers like the one recorded in Mark 16:18, Jesus stated that believers, "...shall lay hands on the sick, and they shall recover." He likewise boldly asserted in Luke 10:19 concerning believers, "Behold, I give unto you power to tread on serpents and scorpions, and over all the power of the enemy: and nothing shall by any means hurt you." (The reference to serpents and scorpions could be interpreted to mean spiritual enemies of God or demonic power.) The believer's authority "over all the power of the enemy" and their role in carrying on the ministry work of Jesus to heal the sick is established by the Word of God.

14. God the Father gave Jesus authority over all things.

Ephesians 1:22-23 And hath put all things under his feet, and gave him to be the head over all things to the church,
Which is his body, the fullness of him that filleth all in all.

Colossians 2:8-10 Beware lest any man spoil you through philosophy and vain deceit, after the tradition of men, after the rudiments of the world, and not after Christ.

For in him dwelleth all the fullness of the Godhead bodily. And ye are complete in him, which is the head of all principality and power:

Matthew 28:18 And Jesus came, and spake unto them, saying, All power is given unto me in heaven and in earth.

John 12:49-50 For I have not spoken of myself; but the Father which sent me, he gave me a commandment, what I should say, and what I should speak.

And I know that his commandment is life everlasting: whatsoever I speak therefore, even as the Father said unto me, so I speak.

John 14:10 Believest thou not that I am in the Father, and the Father in me? the words that I speak unto you, I speak not of myself: but the Father, that dwelleth in me, he doeth the works.

John 14:23-24 Jesus answered and said unto him, If a man love me, he will keep my words: and my Father will love him, and we will come unto him, and make our abode with him.

He that loveth me not, keepeth not my sayings: and the word which ye hear is not mine, but the Father's which sent me.

15. Jesus gave believers authority over all the power of the enemy.

Luke 10:19 Behold, I give unto you power to tread on serpents and scorpions, and over all the power of the enemy: and nothing shall by any means hurt you.

Ephesians 6:12-13 For we wrestle not against flesh and blood, but against principalities, against powers, against the rulers of the darkness of this world, against spiritual wickedness in high places. Wherefore take unto you the whole armour of God, that ye may be able to withstand in the evil day, and having done all, to stand.

James 4:7 Submit yourselves therefore to God. Resist the devil, and he will flee from you.

Romans 8:37 Nay, in all these things we are more than conquerors, through him that loved us.

II Timothy 1:7 For God hath not given us the spirit of fear; but of power, and of love, and of a sound mind.

Matthew 18:18 Verily I say unto you, Whatsoever ye shall bind on earth, shall be bound in heaven: and whatsoever ye shall loose on earth, shall be loosed in heaven.

Matthew 12:29 Or else, how can one enter into a strong man's house, and spoil his goods, except he first bind the strong man? and then he will spoil his house.

Mark 9:23 Jesus said unto him, If thou canst believe, all things are possible to him that believeth.

Matthew 17:20 And Jesus said unto them, Because of your unbelief: for verily I say unto you, If ye have faith as a grain of mustard-seed, ye shall say unto this mountain, Remove hence to yonder place; and it shall remove; and nothing shall be impossible unto you.

Philippians 4:13 I can do all things through Christ, which strengtheneth me.

Matthew 18:19-20 Again I say unto you, That if two of you shall agree on earth, as touching any thing that they shall ask, it shall be done for them of my Father which is in heaven.

For where two or three are gathered together in my name, there am I in the midst of them.

I Timothy 6:12 Fight the good fight of faith, lay hold on eternal life, whereunto thou art also called, and hast professed a good profession before many witnesses.

16. Sickness is of the devil!

Job 2:7 So went Satan forth from the presence of the Lord, and smote Job with sore boils from the sole of his foot unto his crown.

Luke 10:18-19 And he said unto them, I be-held Satan as lightning fall from heaven.

Behold, I give unto you power to tread on serpents and scorpions, and over all the power of the enemy: and nothing shall by any means hurt you.

I John 3:8 He that committeth sin is of the devil; for the devil sinneth from the beginning. For this purpose the Son of God was manifested, that he might destroy the works of the devil.

John 10:10 The thief cometh not, but for to steal, and to kill, and to destroy: I am come that they might have life, and that they might have it more abundantly.

Luke 9:56 For the Son of man is not come to destroy men's lives, but to save them...

Ephesians 6:11-12 Put on the whole armour of God, that ye may be able to stand against the wiles of the devil.

For we wrestle not against flesh and blood, but against principalities, against powers, against the rulers of the darkness of this world, against spiritual wickedness in high places.

I Peter 5:8 Be sober, be vigilant; because your adversary the devil, as a roaring lion, walketh about, seeking whom he may devour.

Acts 10:38 How God anointed Jesus of Nazareth with the Holy Ghost and with power: who went about doing good, and healing all that were oppressed of the devil; for God was with him.

Matthew 8:16 ...they brought unto him many that were possessed with devils: and he cast out the spirits with his word, and healed all that were sick;

Luke 13:11-13 And behold, there was a woman which had a spirit of infirmity eighteen years, and was bowed together, and could in no wise lift up herself.

And when Jesus saw her, he called her to him, and said unto her, Woman, thou art loosed from thine infirmity.

And he laid his hands on her: and immediately she was made straight, and glorified God.

Mark 9:17, 25-27 And one of the multitude answered and said, Master, I have brought unto thee my son, which hath a dumb spirit;

When Jesus saw that the people came running together, he rebuked the foul spirit, saying unto him, Thou dumb and deaf spirit, I charge thee, come out of him, and enter no more into him.

And the spirit cried, and rent him sore, and came out of him: and he was as one dead; insomuch that many said, He is dead.

But Jesus took him by the hand, and lifted him up; and he arose.

Matthew 12:22 Then was brought unto him one possessed with a devil, blind and dumb; and he healed him, insomuch that the blind and dumb both spake and saw.

Luke 4:38-39 And he arose out of the synagogue, and entered into Simon's house. And Simon's wife's mother was taken with a great fever; and they besought him for her.

And he stood over her, and rebuked the fever; and it left her: and immediately she arose and ministered unto them.

Mark 3:10-11 For he had healed many; insomuch that they pressed upon him for to touch him, as many as had plagues.

And unclean spirits, when they saw him, fell down before him, and cried, saying, Thou art the Son of God.

Luke 9:1,6 Then he called his twelve disciples together, and gave them power and authority over all devils, and to cure diseases.

And they departed, and went through the towns, preaching the gospel, and healing every where.

Mark 16:17-18 And these signs shall follow them that believe: In my name shall they cast out devils; they shall speak with new tongues;

They shall take up serpents; and if they drink any deadly thing, it shall not hurt them; they shall lay hands on the sick, and they shall recover.

17. Jesus gave authority and power to believers to minister healing to the sick in His name.

John 17:18 As thou hast sent me into the world, even so have I also sent them into the world.

John 13:20 Verily, verily, I say unto you, He that receiveth whomsoever I send, receiveth me; and he that receiveth me receiveth him that sent me.

Luke 9:1-2 Then he called his twelve disciples together, and gave them power and authority over all devils, and to cure diseases.

And he sent them to preach the kingdom of God, and to heal the sick.

Matthew 10:1, 5, 7-8 And when he had called unto him his twelve disciples, he gave them power against unclean spirits, to cast them out, and to heal all manner of sickness, and all manner of disease.

These twelve Jesus sent forth, and commanded them, saying, Go not into the way of the Gentiles, and into any city of the Samaritans enter ye not.

And as ye go, preach, saying, The kingdom of heaven is at hand. Heal the sick, cleanse the lepers, raise the dead, cast out devils: freely ye have received, freely give.

Mark 3:14-15 And he ordained twelve, that they should be with him, and that he might send them forth to preach,

And to have power to heal sicknesses, and to cast out devils.

Luke 10:1, 8-9 After these things, the Lord appointed other seventy also, and sent them two and two before his face into every city, and place, whither he himself would come.

And into whatsoever city ye enter, and they receive you, eat such things as are set before you.

And heal the sick that are therein, and say unto them, The kingdom of God is come nigh unto you.

Matthew 28:18-20 And Jesus came, and spake unto them, saying, All power is given unto me in heaven and in earth.

Go ye therefore and teach all nations, baptizing them in the name of the Father, and of the Son, and of the Holy Ghost;

Teaching them to observe all things whatsoever I have commanded you: and lo, I am with you alway, even unto the end of the world. Amen.

Mark 16:15-18 And he said unto them, Go ye into all the world, and preach the gospel to every creature.

He that believeth and is baptized, shall be saved; but he that believeth not, shall be damned.

And these signs shall follow them that believe: In my name shall they cast out devils; they shall speak with new tongues; they shall take up serpents; and if they drink any deadly thing, it shall not hurt them;

They shall lay hands on the sick, and they shall recover.

James 5:14-15 Is any sick among you? let him call for the elders of the church; and let them pray over him, anointing him with oil in the name of the Lord:

And the prayer of faith shall save the sick, and the Lord shall raise him up; and if he have committed sins, they shall be forgiven him.

18. Believers have a special relationship with God which enables them to do the works of Jesus which include healings.

John 14:12-14 Verily, verily, I say unto you, He that believeth on me, the works that I do shall he do also; and greater works than these shall he do; because I go unto my Father.

And whatsoever ye shall ask in my name, that will I do, that the Father may be glorified in the Son.

If ye shall ask any thing in my name, I will do it.

Colossians 1:27 To whom God would make known what is the riches of the glory of this mystery among the Gentiles; which is Christ in you, the hope of glory:

Ephesians 2:4-7 But God, who is rich in mercy, for his great love wherewith he loved us,

Even when we were dead in sins, hath quickened us together with Christ; (by grace ye are saved;)

And hath raised us up together, and made us sit together in heavenly places, in Christ Jesus:

That in the ages to come he might shew the exceeding riches of his grace in his kindness toward us, through Christ Jesus.

John 7:37-39 In the last day, that great day of the feast, Jesus stood and cried, saying, If any man thirst, let him come unto me, and drink.

He that believeth on me, as the scripture hath said, out of his belly shall flow rivers of living water.

(But this spake he of the Spirit, which they that believe on him should receive, for the Holy Ghost was not yet given, because that Jesus was not yet glorified.)

John 4:14 But whosoever drinketh of the water that I shall give him, shall never thirst; but the water that I shall give him, shall be in him a well of water springing up into everlasting life.

Luke 24:49 And behold, I send the promise of my Father upon you: but tarry ye in the city of Jerusalem, until ye be endued with power from on high.

Acts 1:8 But ye shall receive power after that the Holy Ghost is come upon you: and ye shall be witnesses unto me, both in Jerusalem, and in all Judea, and in Samaria, and unto the uttermost part of the earth.

Colossians 1:13 Who hath delivered us from the power of darkness, and hath translated us into the kingdom of his dear Son:

Romans 8:14 For as many as are led by the Spirit of God, they are the sons of God.

Galatians 4:7 Wherefore thou art no more a servant, but a son; and if a son, then an heir of God through Christ.

II Corinthian 5:20 Now then we are ambassadors for Christ, as though God did beseech you by us: we pray you in Christ's stead, be ye reconciled to God.

VI

JESUS CHRIST'S FINISHED WORK OF REDEMPTION INCLUDED SALVATION FROM SIN AND SICKNESS.

As a consequence of Adam's temptation by Satan and his rebellion against God in the Garden of Eden, sin and death entered this world. Because Adam was the representative of all future generations, all people thereafter were born with a sin nature. God sent Jesus Christ to set men free from the bonds of that slavery to sin.

The Word of God reveals that Jesus Christ is coexistent with God, partner in creation, the living Word, and the Son of God. He came, being in the form of God, and "...thought it not robbery to be equal with God: But made Himself of no reputation, and took upon him the form of a servant, and was made in the likeness of men: And being found in fashion as a man, he humbled himself, and became obedient unto death, even the death of the cross" (Philippians 2:6-8). I Timothy 2:5-6 records that there is only one who is the "...mediator between God and men, the man Christ Jesus; Who gave himself a ransom for all...". Through the life, death and resurrection of Jesus Christ it is possible for people who are born under the condemnation of sin to be reconciled back to God and receive eternal salvation. Acts 16:31 states, "...Believe on the Lord Jesus Christ, and thou shalt be saved, and thy house."

The salvation which Christ Jesus brought to mankind was a full and complete event. He triumphed over every aspect of the cursed things that came because of Adam's and mankinds' fall into sin. The word salvation when fully understood means deliverance from sin and the terrible effects of sin. One of the "terrible effects of sin" which has the potential to deteriorate and destroy human life is sickness. When salvation came through Jesus Christ, the power of sickness was broken as well as the power of sin.

Divine forgiveness and divine healing are both embodied in the redemption that came through Jesus Christ. He bore our sins (I Peter 2:24) and He bore our sicknesses (Matthew 8:17) so that our sins would be forgiven and our sicknesses healed. Redemption through Jesus Christ's death on the cross and His resurrection was an all encompassing work of salvation. The broadness of this salvation from sin and sickness is most succinctly put in I Peter 2:24 which declares how Jesus "...his own self bare our sins in his own body on the tree, that we, being dead to sins, should live unto righteousness: by whose stripes ye were healed."

Because "Jesus Christ the same yesterday, and to-day, and forever" (Hebrews 13:8) lives even now as our great High Priest and makes intercessions for us (Hebrews 7:25-26), we can confidently turn to Him for the fullness of salvation, which includes forgiveness of sins and healing from sickness.

19. Salvation from sin and the gift of eternal life come through Jesus Christ.

II Peter 3:9 The Lord is not slack concerning his promise, as some men count slackness; but is long-suffering to us-ward, not willing that any should perish, but that all should come to repentance.

John 3:16 For God so loved the world, that he gave his only begotten Son, that whosoever believeth in him should not perish, but have everlasting life.

Romans 1:16 For I am not ashamed of the gospel of Christ: for it is the power of God unto salvation to every one that believeth; to the Jew first, and also to the Greek.

Romans 3:23-26 For all have sinned, and come short of the glory of God;

Being justified freely by his grace, through the redemption that is in Christ Jesus:

Whom God hath set forth to be a propitiation, through faith in his blood, to declare his righteousness for the remission of sins that are past, through the forbearance of God;

To declare, I say, at this time his righteousness: that he might be just, and the justifier of him which believeth in Jesus.

Romans 6:23 For the wages of sin is death: but the gift of God is eternal life, through Jesus Christ our Lord.

Ephesians 1:7 In whom we have redemption through his blood, the forgiveness of sins, according to the riches of his grace;

I Peter 2:24 Who his own self bare our sins in his own body on the tree, that we, being dead to sins, should live unto righteousness: by whose stripes ye were healed.

I John 1:7 But if we walk in the light, as he is in the light, we have fellowship one with another, and the blood of Jesus Christ his Son cleanseth us from all sin.

Acts 16:31 And they said, Believe on the Lord Jesus Christ, and thou shalt be saved, and thy house.

John 3:36 He that believeth on the Son hath everlasting life: and he that believeth not the Son, shall not see life; but the wrath of God abideth on him.

Romans 10:9 That if thou shalt confess with thy mouth the Lord Jesus, and shalt believe in thine heart that God hath raised him from the dead, thou shalt be saved.

II Corinthians 5:17 Therefore, if any man be in Christ, he is a new creature: old things are passed away; behold, all things are become new.

20. Salvation through Jesus Christ includes healing.

Isaiah 53:5 But he was wounded for our transgressions, he was bruised for our iniquities; the chastisement of our peace was upon him; and with his stripes we are healed.

Psalm 103:2-3 Bless the Lord, O my soul, and forget not all his benefits:

Who forgiveth all thine iniquities; who healeth all thy diseases;

Acts 10:38 How God anointed Jesus of Nazareth with the Holy Ghost and with power: who went about doing good, and healing all that were oppressed of the devil; for God was with him.

Matthew 26:26 And as they were eating, Jesus took bread, and blessed it, and brake it, and gave it to the disciples, and said, Take, eat; this is my body.

John 6:56-57 He that eateth my flesh, and drinketh my blood, dwelleth in me, and I in him.

As the living Father hath sent me, and I live by the Father: so he that eateth me, even he shall live by me.

Matthew 8:17 That it might be fulfilled which was spoken by Esaias the prophet, saying, Himself took our infirmities, and bare out sicknesses.

I Peter 2:24 Who his own self bare our sins in his own body on the tree, that we, being dead to sins, should live unto righteousness: by whose stripes ye were healed.

Matthew 12:15 But when Jesus knew it, he withdrew himself from thence: and great multitudes followed him, and he healed them all.

21. Healing through Jesus Christ is available in all ages of time.

Hebrews 13:8 Jesus Christ the same yesterday, and today, and for ever.

John 20:30-31 And many other signs truly did Jesus in the presence of his disciples, which are not written in this book.

But these are written, that ye might believe that Jesus is the Christ, the Son of God; and that believing ye might have life through his name.

Ephesians 5:23 ...Christ is the head of the church: and he is the Saviour of the body.

II Peter 1:3-4 According as his divine power hath given unto us all things that pertain unto life and godliness, through the knowledge of him that hath called us to glory and virtue:

Whereby are given unto us exceeding great and precious promises; that by these ye might be partakers of the divine nature, having escaped the corruption that is in the world through lust.

22. There is no partiality with God. What He is willing to do for one, He will do for another.

> **Psalm 86:5** For thou, Lord, art good, and ready to forgive; and plenteous in mercy unto all them that call upon thee.

> **Romans 2:11** For there is no respect of persons with God.

> **Acts 10:34-36** Then Peter opened his mouth, and said, Of a truth I perceive that God is no respecter of persons:
>
> But in every nation, he that feareth him and worketh righteousness, is accepted with him.
>
> The word which God sent unto the children of Israel, preaching peace by Jesus Christ: (he is Lord of all:)

VII

DIVINE HEALING RELATES TO MANY ASPECTS OF GOD'S RELATIONSHIP TO MANKIND THROUGH JESUS CHRIST

Our heavenly Father has declared boldly and definitively as recorded in Exodus 15:26, "...I am the Lord that healeth thee." Jesus has said, "I am the way, the truth, and the life: no man cometh to the Father, but by me" (John 14:6). These statements reflect the awesome reality underlying divine healing that God our creator and sustainer is ultimately the one from whom healing originates and no one can come to Him except through Jesus Christ, the only begotten Son of God. Jesus Himself declares that He is the way through which mere human beings can reach the Father. He is the embodiment and bearer of absolute truth which directs us to Father God and He is the one through whom we may experience the abundant life. Everything that the Bible has to say about divine healing is an elaboration on, an explanation about and an instruction based on this immovable and unshakable reality.

It must be clearly understood that divine healing is not an isolated phenomenon but one that relates to many aspects of God's relationship with mankind and man's relationship to Him through Jesus Christ. Healing can be impeded, or blocked altogether by numerous things such as a lack of knowledge about God, a lack of awareness of His expectations and a lack of understanding concerning His will regarding healing. Misconceptions, incorrect beliefs, false information about divine healing, sinful behavior, disobedience toward God, and unbelief can also play powerful roles in slowing down or blocking healing from happening. While it is not the scope of this work to illustrate the various ways divine healing can be decelerated, hindered or prevented all together, it is imperative to stress the importance of developing a favorable relationship with God based on God's word and access to God through Jesus Christ.

A few of the more obvious relationship areas concerning healing are recorded here. This section is only a sampling of relationship factors and is given to illustrate the need to delve further into building a wholesome relationship with God based on the knowledge and truth of Jesus Christ. Unless that is done, the honesty of Hosea 4:6 can become an unfortunate reality concerning healing. It ominously warns, "My people are destroyed for lack of knowledge". Let us not be counted in that number!

23. God desires that everyone repent of sin and be cleansed of unrighteousness.

> **II Peter 3:9** The Lord is not slack concerning his promise, as some men count slackness; but is long-suffering to us-ward, not willing that any should perish, but that all should come to repentance.

> **II Corinthians 6:18 and 7:1** And will be a Father unto you, and ye shall be my sons and daughters, saith the Lord Almighty.
> Having therefore these promises, dearly be-

loved, let us cleanse ourselves from all filthiness of the flesh and spirit, perfecting holiness in the fear of God.

James 4:7-8 Submit yourselves therefore to God. Resist the devil, and he will flee from you.

Draw nigh to God, and he will draw nigh to you. Cleanse your hands, ye sinners, and purify your hearts, ye double-minded.

Galatians 5:16-21 This I say then, Walk in the Spirit, and ye shall not fulfil the lust of the flesh.

For the flesh lusteth against the Spirit, and the Spirit against the flesh: and these are contrary the one to the other; so that ye cannot do the things that ye would.

But if ye be led by the Spirit, ye are not under the law.

Now the works of the flesh are manifest, which are these, Adultery, fornication, uncleanness, lasciviousness,

Idolatry, witchcraft, hatred, variance, emulations, wrath, strife, seditions, heresies,

Envyings, murders, drunkenness, revellings, and such like: of the which I tell you before, as I have also told you in time past, that they which do such things shall not inherit the kingdom of God.

Romans 12:1-2 I BESEECH you therefore, brethren, by the mercies of God, that ye present your bodies a living sacrifice, holy, acceptable unto God, which is your reasonable service.

And be not conformed to this world: but be ye transformed by the renewing of your mind, that ye may prove what is that good, and acceptable, and perfect will of God.

I John 1:9 If we confess our sins, he is faithful and just to forgive us our sins, and to cleanse us from all unrighteousness.

24. God is abundant in mercy to forgive.

Psalm 86:5 For thou, Lord, art good, and ready to forgive; and plenteous in mercy unto all them that call upon thee.

Isaiah 43:25-26 I, even I, am he that blotteth out thy transgressions for mine own sake, and will not remember thy sins.

Put me in remembrance: let us plead together: declare thou, that thou mayest be justified.

II Chronicles 7:14 If my people, which are called by my name, shall humble themselves, and pray, and seek my face, and turn from their wicked ways; then will I hear from heaven, and will forgive their sin, and will heal their land.

II Peter 3:9 The Lord is not slack concerning his promise, as some men count slackness; but is long-suffering to us-ward, not willing that any should perish, but that all should come to repentance.

I Peter 3:12 For the eyes of the Lord are over the righteous, and his ears are open unto their prayers: but the face of the Lord is against them that do evil.

Luke 11:9-10 And I say unto you, Ask, and it shall be given you; seek, and ye shall find; knock, and it shall be opened unto you.

For every one that asketh, receiveth; and he that seeketh, findeth; and to him that knocketh, it shall be opened.

25. Forgiveness from sin and unrighteousness comes through Jesus Christ.

I John 1:7 But if we walk in the light, as he is in the light, we have fellowship one with another, and the blood of Jesus Christ his Son cleanseth us from all sin.

Ephesians 1:7 In whom we have redemption through his blood, the forgiveness of sins, according to the riches of his grace;

Colossians 1:14 In whom we have redemption through his blood, even the forgiveness of sins:

I John 1:9 If we confess our sins, he is faithful and just to forgive us our sins, and to cleanse us from all unrighteousness.

Romans 5:19, 21 For as by one man's disobedience many were made sinners, so by the obedience of one shall many be made righteous.

That as sin hath reigned unto death, even so might grace reign through righteousness unto eternal life, by Jesus Christ our Lord.

Matthew 9:5-6 For whether is easier to say, Thy sins be forgiven thee; or to say, Arise, and walk?

But that ye may know that the Son of man hath power on earth to forgive sins, (then saith he to the sick of the palsy,) Arise, take up thy bed, and go unto thine house.

26. A Life of faith in God through Jesus Christ is a life of victory.

I John 5:4 For whatsoever is born of God, overcometh the world: and this is the victory that overcometh the world, even our faith.

Mark 11:22 And Jesus answering, saith unto them, Have faith in God.

II Corinthians 5:7 (For we walk by faith, not by sight:)

II Corinthians 4:18 While we look not at the things which are seen, but at the things which are not seen: for the things which are seen are temporal; but the things which are not seen are eternal.

Romans 10:17 So then, faith cometh by hearing, and hearing by the word of God.

Hebrews 11:1 Now faith is the substance of things hoped for, the evidence of things not seen;

Hebrews 11:6 But without faith it is impossible to please him: for he that cometh to God must believe that he is, and that he is a rewarder of them that diligently seek him.

Romans 12:3 For I say, through the grace given unto me, to every man that is among you, not to think of himself more highly than he ought to think; but to think soberly, according as God hath dealt to every man the measure of faith.

Hebrews 12:2 Looking unto Jesus the author and finisher of our faith; who, for the joy that was set before him, endured the cross, despising the shame, and is set down at the right hand of the throne of God.

Mark 9:23 Jesus said unto him, If thou canst believe, all things are possible to him that believeth.

Galatians 3:5-7 He therefore that ministereth to you the Spirit, and worketh miracles among you, doeth he it by the works of the law, or by the hearing of faith?

Even as Abraham believed God, and it was accounted to him for righteousness.

Know ye therefore, that they which are of faith, the same are the children of Abraham.

Matthew 8:13 And Jesus said unto the centurion, Go thy way; and as thou hast believed, so be it done unto thee. And his servant was healed in the self-same hour.

Mark 5:28-34 For she said, If I may touch but his clothes, I shall be whole.

And straightway the fountain of her blood was dried up; and she felt in her body that she was healed of that plague.

And Jesus, immediately knowing in himself that virtue had gone out of him, turned him about in the press, and said, Who touched my clothes?

And his disciples said unto him, Thou seest the multitude thronging thee, and sayest thou, Who touched me?

And he looked round about to see her that had done this thing.

But the woman, fearing and trembling, knowing what was done in her, came and fell down before him, and told him all the truth.

And he said unto her, Daughter, thy faith hath made thee whole; go in peace, and be whole of they plague.

II Corinthians 13:5 Examine yourselves, whether ye be in the faith; prove your own selves. Know ye not your own selves, how that Jesus Christ is in you, except ye be reprobates?

Colossians 2:6 As ye have therefore received Christ Jesus the Lord, so walk ye in him:

27. Pray to God the Father in the name of Jesus Christ.

Philippians 2:9-10 Wherefore God also hath highly exalted him, and given him a name which is above every name:

That at the name of Jesus every knee should bow, of things in heaven, and things in earth, and things under the earth;

John 3:23 And this is his commandment: That we should believe on the name of his Son Jesus Christ, and love one another, as he gave us commandment.

John 14:13-14 And whatsoever ye shall ask in my name, that will I do, that the Father may be glorified in the Son.

If ye shall ask any thing in my name, I will do it.

John 16:23-24 And in that day ye shall ask me nothing. Verily, verily, I say unto you, Whatsoever ye shall ask the Father in my name, he will give it you.

Hitherto have ye asked nothing in my name: ask, and ye shall receive, that your joy may be full.

Mark 16:17 And these signs shall follow them that believe: In my name shall they cast out devils; they shall speak with new tongues;

Acts 16:18 And this did she many days. But Paul being grieved, turned and said to the spirit,

I command thee in the name of Jesus Christ to come out of her. And he came out the same hour.

Acts 3:6-7 Then Peter said, Silver and gold have I none; but such as I have give I thee: In the name of Jesus Christ of Nazareth, rise up and walk.

And he took him by the right hand, and lifted him up: and immediately his feet and ankle-bones received strength.

Colossians 3:17 And whatsoever ye do in word or deed, do all in the name of the Lord Jesus, giving thanks to God and the Father by him.

Ephesians 5:20 Giving thanks always for all things unto God and the Father, in the name of our Lord Jesus Christ;

Hebrews 13:15 By him therefore let us offer the sacrifice of praise to God continually, that is, the fruit of our lips, giving thanks to his name.

28. Pray according to God's will and keep His commandments.

I John 3:21-22 Beloved, if our heart condemn us not, then have we confidence toward God.

And whatsoever we ask, we receive of him, because we keep his commandments, and do those things that are pleasing in his sight.

I John 5:14-15 And this is the confidence that we have in him, that if we ask anything according to his will, he heareth us:

And if we know that he hear us, whatsoever we ask, we know that we have the petitions that we desired of him.

Philippians 4:6 Be careful for nothing; but in every thing by prayer and supplication with thanksgiving let your requests be made known unto God.

James 4:3 Ye ask, and receive not, because ye ask amiss, that ye may consume it upon your lusts.

29. Pray in believing faith.

Matthew 21:22 And all things whatsoever ye shall ask in prayer, believing, ye shall receive.

Mark 11:24 Therefore I say unto you, What things soever ye desire when ye pray, believe that ye receive them, and ye shall have them.

Mark 11:23 For verily I say unto you, That whosoever shall say unto this mountain, Be thou removed, and be thou cast into the sea; and shall not doubt in his heart, but shall believe that those things which he saith shall come to pass; he shall have whatsoever he saith.

James 5:15 And the prayer of faith shall save the sick, and the Lord shall raise him up; and if he have committed sins, they shall be forgiven him.

James 5:16 Confess your faults one to another, and pray one for another, that ye may be healed. The effectual fervent prayer of a righteous man availeth much.

James 1:6-8 But let him ask in faith, nothing wavering. For he that wavereth is like a wave of the sea driven with the wind and tossed.

For let not that man think that he shall receive any thing of the Lord.

A double-minded man is unstable in all his ways.

Hebrews 11:6 But without faith it is impossible to please him: for he that cometh to God must believe that he is, and that he is a rewarder of them that diligently seek him.

Romans 14:23 And he that doubteth is damned if he eat, because he eateth not of faith: for whatsoever is not of faith is sin.

Romans 10:8 But what saith it? The word is nigh thee, even in thy mouth, and in thy heart: that is, the word of faith, which we preach:

John 15:7 If ye abide in me, and my words abide in you, ye shall ask what ye will, and it shall be done unto you.

Matthew 7:7-8 Ask, and it shall be given you; seek, and ye shall find; knock, and it shall be opened unto you:

For every one that asketh, receiveth; and he that seeketh, findeth; and to him that knocketh, it shall be opened.

Matthew 15:22, 28 And behold, a woman of Canaan came out of the same coasts, and cried unto him, saying, Have mercy on me, O Lord, thou son of David; my daughter is grievously vexed with a devil.

Then Jesus answered and said unto her, O woman, great is thy faith: be it unto thee even as thou wilt. And her daughter was made whole from that very hour.

Matthew 9:29-30 Then touched he their eyes, saying, According to your faith, be it unto you.

And their eyes were opened; and Jesus straitly charged them, saying, See that no man know it.

30. When all is done that can be done, do not shrink back but stand firm in faith.

I Corinthians 16:13 Watch ye, stand fast in the faith, quit you like men, be strong.

Galatians 5:1 Stand fast therefore in the liberty wherewith Christ hath made us free, and be not entangled again with the yoke of bondage.

Hebrews 10:35 Cast not away therefore your confidence, which hath great recompense of reward.

Revelations 3:11 Behold, I come quickly: hold that fast which thou hast, that no man take thy crown.

Ephesians 6:10-17 Finally, my brethren, be strong in the Lord, and in the power of his might.

Put on the whole armour of God, that ye may be able to stand against the wiles of the devil.

For we wrestle not against flesh and blood, but against principalities, against powers, against the rulers of the darkness of this world, against spiritual wickedness in high places.

Wherefore take unto you the whole armour of God, that ye may be able to withstand in the evil day, and having done all, to stand.

Stand therefore, having your loins girt about with truth, and having on the breast-plate of righteousness;

And your feet shod with the preparation of the gospel of peace.

Above all, taking the shield of faith, wherewith ye shall be able to quench all the fiery darts of the wicked.

And take the helmet of salvation, and the sword of the Spirit, which is the word of God.

Hebrews 10:38-39 Now the just shall live by faith: but if any man draw back, my soul shall have no pleasure in him.

But we are not of them who draw back unto perdition; but of them that believe to the saving of the soul.

Hebrews 6:11-12 And we desire that every one of you do shew the same diligence to the full assurance of hope unto the end:

That ye be not slothful, but followers of them who through faith and patience inherit the promises.

James 1:6-8 But let him ask in faith, nothing wavering. For he that wavereth is like a wave of the sea driven with the wind and tossed.

For let not that man think that he shall receive any thing of the Lord.

A double-minded man is unstable in all his ways.

Proverbs 3:5-7 Trust in the Lord with all thine heart; and lean not unto thine own understanding.

In all thy ways acknowledge him, and he shall direct thy paths.

Be not wise in thine own eyes: fear the Lord, and depart from evil.

John 15:4-5 Abide in me, and I in you. As the branch cannot bear fruit of itself, except it abide in the vine: no more can ye, except ye abide in me.

I am the vine, ye are the branches: He that abideth in me, and I in him, the same bringeth forth much fruit: for without me ye can do nothing.

John 15:6-7 If a man abide not in me, he is cast forth as a branch, and is withered; and men gather them, and cast them into the fire, and they are burned.

If ye abide in me, and my words abide in you, ye shall ask what ye will, and it shall be done unto you.

Psalms 25:10 All the paths of the Lord are mercy and truth unto such as keep his covenant and his testimonies.

Psalms 91:14 Because he hath set his love upon me, therefore will I deliver him: I will set him on high, because he hath known my name.

Deuteronomy 7:9 Know therefore that the Lord thy God, he is God, the faithful God, which keepeth covenant and mercy with them that love him and keep his commandments to a thousand generations;

Deuteronomy 28:1 And it shall come to pass, if thou shalt hearken diligently unto the voice of the Lord thy God, to observe and to do all his commandments which I command thee this day: that the Lord thy God will set thee on high above all nations of the earth:

31. Confess Jesus Christ. Confess the Word.

Romans 10:8 But what saith it? The word is nigh thee, even in thy mouth, and in thy heart: that is, the word of faith, which we preach:

Hebrews 3:1 Wherefore, holy brethren, partakers of the heavenly calling, consider the Apostle and High Priest of our profession, Christ Jesus;

Romans 10:13 For whosoever shall call upon the name of the Lord shall be saved.

Romans 10:9 That if thou shalt confess with thy mouth the Lord Jesus, and shalt believe in thine heart that God hath raised him from the dead, thou shalt be saved.

Matthew 10:32-33 Whosoever therefore shall confess me before men, him will I confess also before my Father which is in heaven.

But whosoever shall deny me before men, him will I also deny before my Father which is in heaven.

Hebrews 10:23 Let us hold fast the profession of our faith without wavering; for he is faithful that promised:

Hebrews 4:14 Seeing then that we have a great High Priest, that is passed into the heavens, Jesus the Son of God, let us hold fast our profession.

Revelations 12:11 And they overcame him by the blood of the Lamb, and by the word of their testimony; and they loved not their lives unto the death.

Matthew 15:11 Not that which goeth into the mouth defileth a man; but that which cometh out of the mouth, this defileth a man.

Matthew 12:37 For by thy words thou shalt be justified, and by thy words thou shalt be condemned.

Proverbs 18:21 Death and life are in the power of the tongue: and they that love it shall eat the fruit thereof.

Proverbs 21:23 Whoso keepeth his mouth and his tongue, keepeth his soul from troubles.

Proverbs 16:24 Pleasant words are as an honeycomb, sweet to the soul, and health to the bones.

Proverbs 4:20-22 My son, attend to my words; incline thine ear unto my sayings.

Let them not depart from thine eyes; keep them in the midst of thine heart.

For they are life unto those that find them, and health to all their flesh.

VIII

GOD USES A VARIETY OF METHODS
TO HEAL

"...With God all things are possible" (Matthew 19:26). In light of this profound actuality, it should not be surprising that in the domain of divine healing God is not limited in His methods and resources for healing. From Jesus spitting on the ground and anointing the blind man's eyes with the saliva moistened clay (John 9:6) to the most advanced medical procedures, God has healed people.

While God remains unlimited in His resources for healing, the Bible records a number of specific methods through which healing has come. The most common and frequently referred to Biblical methods of divine healing are listed here in this section. Since their inception, these methods for healing have become examples for prayer and theory regarding divine healing. Some are actually appointed by Jesus for believers to engage in as exemplified by the charge given in Mark 16:17-18 that believers will "lay hands on the sick" so that they will recover and His strong command to "cast out devils" (Matthew 10:8).

Jesus Christ is the model for all believers and "All scripture is given by inspiration of God, and is profitable for doctrine, for reproof, for correction, for instruction in righteousness: That the man of God may be complete, thoroughly furnished unto all good works" (II Timothy 3:16-17). The methods of ministering divine healing instructed by Jesus and those recorded in Scripture by inspiration of God remain valid ways through which divine healing can come. We must remember, however, that God is not limited to, nor restricted by, any one or all of these means because He is infinitely resourceful and "...with God nothing shall be impossible" (Luke 1:37).

32. Healing can come by the method of "laying on of hands" by a believer.

> **Luke 4:40** Now when the sun was setting, all they that had any sick with divers diseases, brought them unto him: and he laid his hands on every one of them, and healed them.

> **Luke 13:11-13** And behold, there was a woman which had a spirit of infirmity eighteen years, and was bowed together, and could in no wise lift up herself.
> And when Jesus saw her, he called her to him, and said unto her, Woman, thou art loosed from thine infirmity.
> And he laid his hands on her: and immediately she was made straight, and glorified God.

> **Matthew 9:27, 29, 30** And when Jesus departed thence, two blind men followed him, crying, and saying, Thou son of David, have mercy on us.
> Then touched he their eyes, saying, According to your faith, be it unto you.
> And their eyes were opened; and Jesus straitly charged them, saying, See that no man know it.

Mark 7:32 And they bring unto him one that was deaf, and had an impediment in his speech; and they beseech him to put his hand upon him.

Mark 5:22-23 And behold, there cometh one of the rulers of the synagogue, Jairus by name; and when he saw him, he fell at his feet,

And besought him greatly, saying, My little daughter lieth at the point of death: I pray thee, come and lay thy hands on her, that she may be healed; and she shall live.

Mark 16:15-18 And he said unto them, Go ye into all the world, and preach the gospel to every creature.

He that believeth and is baptized, shall be saved; but he that believeth not, shall be damned.

And these signs shall follow them that believe: In my name shall they cast out devils; they shall speak with new tongues;

They shall take up serpents; and if they drink any deadly thing, it shall not hurt them; they shall lay hands on the sick, and they shall recover.

Acts 9:15-18 But the Lord said unto him, Go thy way: for he is a chosen vessel unto me, to bear my name before the Gentiles, and kings, and the children of Israel.

For I will shew him how great things he must suffer for my name's sake.

And Ananias went his way, and entered into the house: and putting his hands on him, said,

Brother Saul, the Lord (even Jesus that appeared unto thee in the way as thou camest) hath sent me, that thou mightest receive thy sight, and be filled with the Holy Ghost.

And immediately there fell from his eyes as it had been scales: and he received sight forthwith, and arose, and was baptized.

Acts 28:8 And it came to pass, that the father of Publius lay sick of a fever, and of a bloody-flux: to whom Paul entered in, and prayed, and laid his hands on him, and healed him.

Hebrews 6:1-2 Therefore leaving the principles of the doctrine of Christ, let us go on unto perfection; not laying again the foundation of repentance from dead works, and of faith toward God,

Of the doctrine of baptisms, and of laying on of hands, and of resurrection of the dead, and of eternal judgment.

Mark 6:4-6 But Jesus said unto them, A prophet is not without honour, but in his own country, and among his own kin, and in his own house.

And he could there do no mighty work, save that he laid his hands upon a few sick folk, and healed them.

And he marvelled because of their unbelief. And he went round about the villages teaching.

33. Healing can come through the prayer of faith and intercessory prayer.

James 5:14-15 Is any sick among you? let him call for the elders of the church; and let them pray over him, anointing him with oil in the name of the Lord:

And the prayer of faith shall save the sick, and the Lord shall raise him up; and if he have committed sins, they shall be forgiven him.

James 5:16 Confess your faults one to another, and pray one for another, that ye may be healed. The effectual fervent prayer of a righteous man availeth much.

Mark 11:24 Therefore I say unto you, What things soever ye desire when ye pray, believe that ye receive them, and ye shall have them.

Matthew 21:22 And all things whatsoever ye shall ask in prayer, believing, ye shall receive.

Matthew 17:20 And Jesus said unto them, Because of your unbelief: for verily I say unto you, If ye have faith as a grain of mustard-seed, ye shall say unto this mountain, Remove hence to yonder place; and it shall remove; and nothing shall be impossible unto you.

Matthew 8:8 The centurion answered and said, Lord, I am not worthy that thou shouldest come under my roof: but speak the word only, and my servant shall be healed.

John 15:7 If ye abide in me, and my words abide in you, ye shall ask what ye will, and it shall be done unto you.

I John 5:4 For whatsoever is born of God, overcometh the world: and this is the victory that overcometh the world, even our faith.

34. Healing can occur when a believer anoints the sick person with a substance which most commonly is anointing oil.

Mark 6:12-13 And they went out, and preached that men should repent.

And they cast out many devils, and anointed with oil many that were sick, and healed them.

James 5:14 Is any sick among you? let him call for the elders of the church; and let them pray over him, anointing him with oil in the name of the Lord:

John 9:11 He answered and said, A man that is called Jesus, made clay, and anointed mine eyes, and said unto me, Go to the pool of Siloam, and wash: and I went and washed, and I received sight.

Leviticus 8:10-12 And Moses took the anointing oil, and anointed the tabernacle and all that was therein, and sanctified them.

And he sprinkled thereof upon the altar seven times, and anointed the altar and all his vessels, both the laver and his foot, to sanctify them.

And he poured of the anointing oil upon Aaron's head, and anointed him, to sanctify him.

35. When sickness is caused by an evil spirit, healing can come by casting out that spirit.

Matthew 8:16-17 When the even was come, they brought unto him many that were possessed with devils: and he cast out the spirits with his word, and healed all that were sick;

That it might be fulfilled which was spoken by Esaias the prophet, saying, Himself took our infirmities, and bare our sicknesses.

Matthew 9:32-33 As they went out, behold, they brought to him a dumb man possessed with a devil.

And when the devil was cast out, the dumb spake: and the multitudes marvelled, saying, It was never so seen in Israel.

Matthew 12:22 Then was brought unto him one possessed with a devil, blind and dumb; and he healed him, insomuch that the blind and dumb both spake and saw.

Mark 9:25 When Jesus saw that the people came running together, he rebuked the foul spirit, saying unto him, Thou dumb and deaf spirit, I charge thee, come out of him, and enter no more into him.

Luke 4:33, 35 And in the synagogue there was a man which had a spirit of an unclean devil; and he cried out with a loud voice,

And Jesus rebuked him, saying, Hold thy

peace, and come out of him. And when the devil had thrown him in the midst, he came out of him, and hurt him not.

Luke 4:36 And they were all amazed, and spake among themselves, saying, What a word is this! for with authority and power he commandeth the unclean spirits, and they come out.

Luke 9:1 The he called his twelve disciples together, and gave them power and authority over all devils, and to cure diseases.

Ephesians 6:12 For we wrestle not against flesh and blood, but against principalities, against powers, against the rulers of the darkness of this world, against spiritual wickedness in high places.

Matthew 10:8 Heal the sick, cleanse the lepers, raise the dead, cast out devils: freely ye have received, freely give.

Mark 16:17 And these signs shall follow them that believe: In my name shall they cast out devils; they shall speak with new tongues;

Matthew 12:28-29 But if I cast out devils by the Spirit of God, then the kingdom of God is come unto you.

Or else, how can one enter into a strong man's house, and spoil his goods, except he first bind the strong man? and then he will spoil his house.

Matthew 18:18 Verily I say unto you, Whatsoever ye shall bind on earth, shall be bound in heaven: and whatsoever ye shall loose on earth, shall be loosed in heaven.

36. Healing can come by speaking to the sickness problem or sick person in commanding faith.

Matthew 28:18 And Jesus came, and spake unto them, saying, All power is given unto me in heaven and in earth.

Mark 11:23 For verily I say unto you, That whosoever shall say unto this mountain, Be thou removed, and be thou cast into the sea; and shall not doubt in his heart, but shall believe that those things which he saith shall come to pass; he shall have whatsoever he saith.

Luke 17:6 And the Lord said, If ye had faith as a grain of mustard-seed, ye might say unto this sycamine-tree, Be thou plucked up by the root, and be thou planted in the sea; and it should obey you.

Matthew 17:19-20 Then came the disciples to Jesus apart, and said, Why could not we cast him out?

And Jesus said unto them, Because of your unbelief: for verily I say unto you, If ye have faith as a grain of mustard-seed, ye shall say unto this mountain, Remove hence to yonder place; and it shall remove; and nothing shall be impossible unto you.

Matthew 8:16-17 When the even was come, they brought unto him many that were possessed with devils: and he cast out the spirits with his word, and healed all that were sick;

That it might be fulfilled which was spoken by Esaias the prophet, saying, Himself took our infirmities, and bare our sicknesses.

Mark 9:25-26 When Jesus saw that the people came running together, he rebuked the foul spirit, saying unto him, Thou dumb and deaf spirit, I charge thee, come out of him, and enter no more into him.

And the spirit cried, and rent him sore, and came out of him: and he was as one dead; insomuch that many said, He is dead.

Luke 4:36 And they were all amazed, and spake among themselves, saying, What a word is this! for with authority and power he commandeth the unclean spirits, and they come out.

John 9:7 And said unto him, Go, wash in the pool of Siloam, (which is by interpretation, Sent.) He went his way therefore, and washed, and came seeing.

John 5:8-9 Jesus saith unto him, Rise, take up thy bed, and walk.

And immediately the man was made whole, and took up his bed, and walked: and on the same day was the sabbath.

Matthew 12:10, 13 And behold, there was a man which had his hand withered. And they asked him, saying, Is it lawful to heal on the sabbath-days? that they might accuse him.

Then saith he to the man, Stretch forth thine hand. And he stretched it forth; and it was restored whole, like as the other.

37. Healing can come when faith is put into action.

Luke 17:12,14 And as he entered into a certain village, there met him ten men that were lepers, which stood afar off:

And when he saw them, he said unto them, Go shew yourselves unto the priests. And it came to pass, that, as they went, they were cleansed.

John 9:6-7 When he had thus spoken, he spat on the ground, and made clay of the spittle, and he anointed the eyes of the blind man with the clay,

And said unto him, Go, wash in the pool of Siloam, (which is by, interpretation, Sent.) He went his way therefore, and washed, and came seeing.

Mark 2:4-5, 11-12 And when they could not come nigh unto him for the press, they uncovered the roof where he was: and when they had broken it up, they let down the bed wherein the sick of the palsy lay.

When Jesus saw their faith, he said unto the sick of the palsy, Son, thy sins be forgiven thee.

I say unto thee, Arise, and take up thy bed, and go thy way into thine house,

And immediately he arose, took up the bed, and went forth before them all; insomuch that they were all amazed, and glorified God, saying, We never saw it on this fashion.

Matthew 8:13 And Jesus said unto the centurion, Go thy way; and as thou hast believed, so be it done unto thee. And his servant was healed in the self-same hour.

Mark 3:5 And when he had looked round about on them with anger, being grieved for the hardness of their hearts, he saith unto the man, Stretch forth thine hand. And he stretched it out: and his hand was restored whole as the other.

James 2:17 Even so faith, if it hath not works, is dead, being alone.

James 2:22 Seest thou how faith wrought with his works, and by works was faith made perfect?

Colossians 2:6 As ye have therefore received Christ Jesus the Lord, so walk ye in him:

38. Healing can come when requested of God in believing faith in the name of Jesus Christ.

Acts 10:38 How God anointed Jesus of Nazareth with the Holy Ghost and with power: who went about doing good, and healing all that were oppressed of the devil; for God was with him.

John 14:12 Verily, verily, I say unto you, He that believeth on me, the works that I do shall he do also; and greater works than these shall he do; because I go unto my Father.

John 14:13 And whatsoever ye shall ask in my name, that will I do, that the Father may be glorified in the Son.

John 14:14 If ye shall ask any thing in my name, I will do it.

John 15:7 If ye abide in me, and my words abide in you, ye shall ask what ye will, and it shall be done unto you.

Mark 16:17 And these signs shall follow them that believe: In my name shall they cast out devils; they shall speak with new tongues;

Acts 3:6-7 Then Peter said, Silver and gold have I none; but such as I have give I thee: In the name of Jesus Christ of Nazareth, rise up and walk.
And he took him by the right hand, and lifted him up: and immediately his feet and ancle-bones received strength.

Acts 4:29-30 And now, Lord, behold their threatenings: and grant unto thy servants, that with all boldness they may speak thy word,

By stretching forth thine hand to heal; and that signs and wonders may be done by the name of thine holy child Jesus.

Colossians 3:17 And whatsoever ye do in word or deed, do all in the name of the Lord Jesus, giving thanks to God and the Father by him.

39. Healing can come when the prayer of agreement is prayed.

Matthew 18:19-20 Again I say unto you, That if two of you shall agree on earth, as touching any thing that they shall ask, it shall be done for them of my Father which is in heaven.
   For where two or three are gathered together in my name, there am I in the midst of them.

I Corinthians 1:10, 13 Now I beseech you, brethren, by the name of our Lord Jesus Christ, that ye all speak the same thing, and that there be no divisions among you; but that ye be perfectly joined together in the same mind, and in the same judgment.
   Is Christ divided? was Paul crucified for you? or were ye baptized in the name of Paul?

Luke 10:1 After these things, the Lord appointed other seventy also, and sent them two and two before his face into every city, and place, whither he himself would come.

Leviticus 26:8 And five of you shall chase an hundred, an hundred of you shall put ten thousand to flight: and your enemies shall fall before you by the sword.

Deuteronomy 32:30 How should one chase a thousand, and two put ten thousand to flight, except their Rock had sold them, and the Lord had shut them up?

Ecclesiastes 4:9,12 Two are better than one; because they have a good reward for their labour.

And if one prevail against him, two shall withstand him; and a threefold cord is not quickly broken.

40. Healing can come when a sick person comes into the presence of a believer who is highly anointed by God for ministering healing or has touched garments he has worn or objects he has handled. This was exemplified by Jesus, the apostles Paul and Peter, and even the bones of Elisha.

Mark 6:56 And whithersoever he entered, into villages, or cities, or country, they laid the sick in the streets, and besought him that they might touch, if it were but the border of his garment: and as many as touched him, were made whole.

Matthew 14:34-36 And when they were gone over, they came into the land of Gennesaret.

And when the men of that place had knowledge of him, they sent out into all that country round about, and brought unto him all that were diseased;

And besought him that they might only touch

the hem of his garment: and as many as touched were made perfectly whole.

Mark 5:25-30, 33-34 And a certain woman which had an issue of blood twelve years,

And had suffered many things of many physicians, and had spent all that she had, and was nothing bettered, but rather grew worse,

When she had heard of Jesus, came in the press behind, and touched his garment:

For she said, If I may touch but his clothes, I shall be whole. And straightway the fountain of her blood was dried up; and she felt in her body that she was healed of that plague.

And Jesus, immediately knowing in himself that virtue had gone out of him, turned him about in the press, and said, Who touched my clothes?

But the woman, fearing and trembling, knowing what was done in her, came and fell down before him, and told him all the truth.

And he said unto her, Daughter, thy faith hath made thee whole; go in peace, and be whole of thy plague.

Acts 19:11,12 And God wrought special miracles by the hands of Paul:

So that from his body were brought unto the sick handkerchiefs, or aprons, and the diseases departed from them, and the evil spirits went out of them.

Acts 5:12, 15-16 And by the hands of the apostles were many signs and wonders wrought among the people; and they were all of one accord in Solomon's porch.

Insomuch that they brought forth the sick into the streets, and laid them on beds and couches, that at the least the shadow of Peter passing by might overshadow some of them.

There came also a multitude out of the cities round about unto Jerusalem, bringing sick folks, and them which were vexed with unclean spirits; and they were healed every one.

II Kings 13:21 And it came to pass, as they were burying a man, that behold, they spied a band of men; and they cast the man into the sepulchre of Elisha: and when the man was let down, and touched the bones of Elisha, he revived, and stood up on his feet.

41. Healing can come by believing, trusting, remaining faithful to, and confessing God's Word and healing promises.

Romans 10:8 But what saith it? The word is nigh thee, even in thy mouth, and in thy heart: that is, the word of faith, which we preach:

Romans 1:16 For I am not ashamed of the gospel of Christ: for it is the power of God unto salvation to every one that believeth; to the Jew first, and also to the Greek.

Psalm 107:20 He sent his word, and healed them, and delivered them from their destructions.

Isaiah 55:11 So shall my word be that goeth forth out of my mouth: it shall not return unto me void, but it shall accomplish that which I please, and it shall prosper in that thing whereto I sent it.

Jeremiah 1:12 Then said the Lord unto me, Thou hast well see: for I will hasten my word to perform it.

I Kings 8:56 Blessed be the Lord, that hath given rest unto his people Israel, according to all that he promised: there hath not failed one word of all his good promise, which he promised by the hand of Moses his servant.

Proverbs 4:20-22 My son, attend to my words; incline thine ear unto my sayings.

Let them not depart from thine eyes; keep them in the midst of thine heart.

For they are life unto those that find them, and health to all their flesh.

Proverbs 18:21 Death and life are in the power of the tongue: and they that love it shall eat the fruit thereof.

Proverbs 12:18 There is that speaketh like the piercings of a sword: but the tongue of the wise is health.

Hebrews 4:14 Seeing then that we have a great High Priest, that is passed into the heavens, Jesus the Son of God, let us hold fast our profession.

Hebrews 10:23 Let us hold fast the profession of our faith without wavering; for he is faithful that promised:

Revelations 12:11 And they overcame him by the blood of the Lamb, and by the word of their testimony; and they loved not their lives unto the death.

Ephesians 4:29 Let no corrupt communication proceed out of your mouth, but that which is good to the use of edifying, that it may minister grace unto the hearers.

Philippians 4:8 Finally, brethren, whatsoever things are true, whatsoever things are honest, whatsoever things are just, whatsoever things are pure, whatsoever things are lovely, whatsoever things are of good report; if there be any virtue, and if there be any praise, think on these things.

42. Healing can come through communion, the Lord's Supper, when properly discerned and taken in a worthy manner.

John 6:56-57 He that eateth my flesh, and drinketh my blood, dwelleth in me, and I in him.

As the living Father hath sent me, and I live by the Father: so he that eateth me, even he shall live by me.

Matthew 26:26 And as they were eating, Jesus took bread, and blessed it, and brake it, and gave it to the disciples, and said, Take, eat; this is my body.

Isaiah 53:5 But he was wounded for our transgressions, he was bruised for our iniquities; the chastisement of our peace was upon him; and with his stripes we are healed.

Matthew 8:17 That it might be fulfilled which was spoken by Esaias the prophet, saying, Himself took our infirmities, and bare our sicknesses.

Matthew 26:27-28 And he took the cup, and gave thanks, and gave it to them, saying, Drink ye all of it;
For this is my blood of the new testament, which is shed for many for the remission of sins.

I Peter 2:24 Who his own self bare our sins in his own body on the tree, that we, being dead to sins, should live unto righteousness: by whose stripes ye were healed.

I Corinthians 11:23-24 For I have received of the Lord, that which also I delivered unto you, That the Lord Jesus, the same night in which he was betrayed, took bread:
And when he had given thanks, he brake it, and said, Take, eat: this is my body, which is broken for you: this do in remembrance of me.

43. Healing can come through God using doctors, medicine, medical procedures and natural laws.

> **Matthew 9:12** But when Jesus heard that, he said unto them, They that be whole need not a physician, but they that are sick.

> **Proverbs 17:22** A merry heart doeth good like a medicine: but a broken spirit drieth the bones.

> **Colossians 4:14** Luke, the beloved physician, and Demas, greet you.

> **II Kings 20:7** And Isaiah said, Take a lump of figs. And they took and laid it on the boil, and he recovered.

> **Acts 27:33-34** And while the day was coming on, Paul besought them all to take meat, saying, This day is the fourteenth day that ye have tarried, and continued fasting, having taken nothing.
>   Wherefore I pray you to take some meat; for this is for your health: for there shall not an hair fall from the head of any of you.

> **Jeremiah 8:22** Is there no balm in Gilead; is there no physician there? why then is not the health of the daughter of my people recovered?

> **Genesis 50:2** And Joseph commanded his servants the physicians to embalm his father: and the physicians embalmed Israel.

Leviticus 13-15 (These chapters give examples of Old Testament methods for dealing with certain types of diseases.)

IX

THE HOLY SPIRIT PLAYS A VITAL ROLE IN DIVINE HEALING

The role of the Holy Spirit in divine healing is vitally profound but hardly unexpected when you consider the fact that the Holy Spirit, as the third person of the trinity, is coexistent with the Father and the Son and functions in complete harmony and union with them. The Holy Spirit exercises the power of the Father and of the Son as exemplified by His participation in such awesome events as creation (Genesis 1:2), the incarnation of Jesus Christ (Luke 1:30-35), the empowerment of Jesus Christ (Matthew 12:28-29; Luke 11:20; Acts 10:38) and the resurrection of Jesus Christ (Romans 8:11). He, likewise, is the powerful participant in the redemption of mankind who convicts of sin, righteousness and judgement (John 16:5-11). The Holy Spirit enables spiritual regeneration in the "new birth" (John 3:3-8), guides believers in their walk with God (John 16:13-15) and ministers to them (John 14:16, 26). In all of these works, and countless others like them, the Holy Spirit has moved in complete accord with the Father and the Son from the very beginning. He has continued to move with them throughout all time and will continue to do so even beyond the final moments of this present age (Revelations 22:17).

Specific to divine healing the important empowerment of the Holy Spirit can be clearly seen. Jesus Himself credited the Holy Spirit as the power by which He cast out demons

(Matthew 12:28-29) and Acts 10:38 reveals "How God anointed Jesus of Nazareth with the Holy Ghost and with power: who went about doing good and healing all that were oppressed of the devil..."

Not only was Jesus empowered by the Holy Spirit for His ministry work, which included healing the sick, but when He instructed believers to continue doing the work He did, He prepared them to receive Holy Spirit empowerment (John 14:12, 16-17; Mark 16:15-18). Just moments before His ascension to the Father, Jesus instructed His disciples to tarry in Jerusalem to receive the Promise of the Father, who is the Holy Spirit, and to be "...endued with power from on high." (Luke 24:49; Acts 1:4-5). With that empowerment of the Holy Spirit (Acts 1:5,8; Acts 2:4) came the gifts of the Spirit including those related to healing (I Corinthians 12:1-11).

Indeed, the Holy Spirit equipped Jesus' disciples to continue His ministry to the sick and He equips believers today to do the same (Acts 2:39; Hebrews 13:8; John 17:20). He enables that work to go forth and empowers them to fulfill Mark 16:18 which says they shall "...lay hands on the sick, and they shall recover."

44. The Holy Spirit participated in creation.

> **Genesis 1:2** And the earth was without form, and void; and darkness was upon the face of the deep: and the Spirit of God moved upon the face of the waters.

45. The Holy Spirit was with Jesus in a powerful way.

Matthew 3:16 And Jesus, when he was baptized, went up straightway out of the water: and lo, the heavens were opened unto him, and he saw the Spirit of God descending like a dove, and lighting upon him:

Luke 4:17-19, 21 And there was delivered unto him the book of the prophet Esaias. And when he had opened the book, he found the place where it was written,

The Spirit of the Lord is upon me, because he hath anointed me to preach the gospel to the poor; he hath sent me to heal the broken-hearted, to preach deliverance to the captives, and recovering of sight to the blind, to set at liberty them that are bruised,

To preach the acceptable year of the Lord.

And he began to say unto them, This day is this scripture fulfilled in your ears.

Acts 10:38 ...God anointed Jesus of Nazareth with the Holy Ghost and with power: who went about doing good, and healing all that were oppressed of the devil; for God was with him.

46. Jesus proclaimed the Holy Spirit of God.

Matthew 12:28 But if I cast out devils by the Spirit of God, then the kingdom of God is come unto you.

John 3:5 Jesus answered, Verily, verily, I say unto thee, Except a man be born of water, and of the Spirit, he cannot enter into the kingdom of God.

47. Jesus promised to send the Holy Spirit to be the Helper to believers.

John 16:7-8 Nevertheless, I tell you the truth: It is expedient for you that I go away: for if I go not away the Comforter well not come unto you; but if I depart, I will send him unto you.

And when he is come, he will reprove the world of sin, and of righteousness, and of judgment:

John 16:13-15 Howbeit, when he, the Spirit of truth, is come, he will guide you into all truth: for he shall not speak of himself; but whatsoever he shall hear, that shall he speak: and he will shew you things to come.

He shall glorify me: for he shall receive of mine, and shall shew it unto you.

All things that the Father hath are mine: therefore said I, that he shall take of mine, and shall shew it unto you.

John 14:26 But the Comforter, which is the Holy Ghost, whom the Father will send in my name, he shall teach you all things, and bring all things to your remembrance, whatsoever I have said unto you.

48. Jesus sent the promised Holy Spirit to endue believers with power and provide spiritual gifts including the gifts of healings.

Luke 24:49 And behold, I send the promise of my Father upon you: but tarry ye in the city of Jerusalem, until ye be endued with power from on high.

Acts 1:8 But ye shall receive power after that the Holy Ghost is come upon you: and ye shall be witnesses unto me, both in Jerusalem, and in all Judea, and in Samaria, and unto the uttermost part of the earth.

Acts 2:4 And they were all filled with the Holy Ghost, and began to speak with other tongues, as the Spirit gave them utterance.

I Corinthians 12:4, 8-11 Now there are diversities of gifts, but the same Spirit.

For to one is given by the Spirit the word of wisdom; to another, the word of knowledge by the same Spirit;

To another, faith by the same Spirit; to another, the gifts of healing by the same Spirit;

To another, the working of miracles; to another, prophecy; to another, discerning of spirits; to another, divers kinds of tongues; to another, the interpretation of tongues:

But all these worketh that one and the selfsame Spirit, dividing to every man severally as he will.

Mark 16:16-18 He that believeth and is baptized, shall be saved; but he that believeth not, shall be damned.

And these signs shall follow them that believe: In my name shall they cast out devils; they shall speak with new tongues;

They shall take up serpents; and if they drink any deadly thing, it shall not hurt them; they shall lay hands on the sick, and they shall recover.

Hebrews 2:3-4 How shall we escape, if we neglect so great salvation; which at the first began to be spoken by the Lord, and was confirmed unto us by them that heard him;

God also bearing them witness, both with signs and wonders, and with divers miracles, and gifts of the Holy Ghost, according to his own will?

I Corinthians 12:27, 28 Now ye are the body of Christ, and members in particular.

And God hath set some in the church, first apostles, secondarily prophets, thirdly teachers, after that miracles, then gifts of healings, helps, governments, diversities of tongues.

49. God is Spirit. The Lord is the Spirit. The Spirit indwelling believers gives life.

John 4:24 God is a Spirit...

II Corinthians 3:17 Now the Lord is that Spirit: and where the Spirit of the Lord is, there is liberty.

Romans 8:11 But if the Spirit of him that raised up Jesus from the dead dwell in you, he that raised up Christ from the dead shall also quicken your mortal bodies by his Spirit that dwelleth in you.

X

BELIEVERS HAVE AN IMPORTANT RESPONSE TO GOD CONCERNING HEALING

All that God has ever done, is doing, or ever will do is from the depth of His love which surpasses all understanding and is perfect in every way. From God's essential nature of love (I John 4:8) comes His high regard for His human children. Salvation from sin and healing are two outstanding expressions of the outpouring of His love toward humankind.

The natural response of a believer who has been delivered "...from the power of darkness" and has been "...translated into the kingdom of his dear Son..." (Colossians 1:13) and who is the recipient of "...all spiritual blessings..." (Ephesians 1:3) would be that of complete, uninhibited devotion and love. Jesus Christ summed it up with these words as recorded in Matthew 22:37, "...Thou shalt love the Lord thy God with all thy heart, with all thy soul, and with all thy mind."

I John 1:3,6-7 states, "...our fellowship is with the Father, and with his Son Jesus Christ...If we say we have fellowship with him, and walk in darkness, we lie, and do not the truth: But if we walk in the light, as he is in the light, we have fellowship one with another, and the blood of Jesus Christ his Son cleanseth us from all sin."

A life lived uprightly before God filled with praise, worship and thanksgiving to Him through Jesus Christ is not only in accordance with God's will for mankind and pleasing in His sight, but is the believer's response to the loving, saving and healing grace of God. Such a life plays an important role in receiving healing and living in divine health.

50. Walk uprightly before the Lord.

Proverbs 3:7 Be not wise in thine own eyes: fear the Lord, and depart from evil.

Psalms 84:11 For the Lord God is a sun and shield: the Lord will give grace and glory; no good thing will he withhold from them that walk uprightly.

II Timothy 2:15 Study to shew thyself approved unto God, a workman that needeth not to be ashamed, rightly dividing the word of truth.

I John 2:6 He that saith he abideth in him, ought himself also so to walk, even as he walked.

Galatians 5:16-21 This I say then, Walk in the Spirit, and ye shall not fulfil the lust of the flesh.

For the flesh lusteth against the Spirit, and the Spirit against the flesh: and these are contrary the one to the other; so that ye cannot do the things that ye would.

But if ye be led by the Spirit, ye are not under the law.

Now the works of the flesh are manifest, which are these; Adultery, fornication, uncleanness, lasciviousness,

Idolatry, witchcraft, hatred, variance, emulations, wrath, strife, seditions, heresies,

Envyings, murders, drunkenness, revellings, and such like: of the which I tell you before, as I have also told you in time past, that they which do such things shall not inherit the kingdom of God.

Malachi 4:2 But unto you that fear my name, shall the Sun of righteousness arise with healing in his wings; and ye shall go forth, and grow up as calves of the stall.

Romans 12:1 I BESEECH you therefore, brethren, by the mercies of God, that ye present your bodies a living sacrifice, holy, acceptable unto God, which is your reasonable service.

Psalms 37:4 Delight thyself also in the Lord; and he shall give thee the desires of thine heart.

Matthew 5:16 Let your light so shine before men, that they may see your good works, and glorify your Father which is in heaven.

Malachi 3:10 Bring ye all the tithes into the storehouse, that there may be meat in mine house, and prove me now herewith, saith the Lord of hosts, if I will not open you the windows of heaven, and pour you out a blessing, that there shall not be room enough to receive it.

51. Praise and worship God offering thanksgiving in the name of Jesus Christ.

Hebrews 13:15 By him therefore let us offer the sacrifice of praise to God continually, that is, the fruit of our lips, giving thanks to his name.

Psalm 50:14,15 Offer unto God thanksgiving; and pay thy vows unto the Most High:
And call upon me in the day of trouble: I will deliver thee, and thou shalt glorify me.

I Peter 2:9 But ye are a chosen generation, a royal priesthood, an holy nation, a peculiar people; that ye should shew forth the praises of him who hath called you out of darkness into his marvelous light:

I Corinthians 15:57 But thanks be to God, which giveth us the victory, through our Lord Jesus Christ.

Psalm 67:5-6 Let the people praise thee, O God; let all the people praise thee.
Then shall the earth yield her increase; and God, even our own God, shall bless us.

I Thessalonians 5:16-18 Rejoice evermore.
Pray without ceasing.
In every thing give thanks: for this is the will of God in Christ Jesus concerning you.

Psalm 113:3 From the rising of the sun unto the going down of the same the Lord's name is to be praised.

Psalm 136:1 O Give thanks unto the Lord; for he is good: for his mercy endureth for ever.

Psalm 100:1-5 Make a joyful noise unto the Lord, all ye lands.

Serve the Lord with gladness: come before his presence with singing.

Know ye that the Lord he is God: it is he that hath made us, and not we ourselves; we are his people, and the sheep of his pasture.

Enter into his gates with thanksgiving, and into his courts with praise: be thankful unto him, and bless his name.

For the Lord is good; his mercy is everlasting; and his truth endureth to all generations.